ROHIT SHARMA

JUGGERNAUT BOOKS
C-I-128, First Floor, Sangam Vihar, Near Holi Chowk,
New Delhi 110080, India

First published by Juggernaut Books 2025

Copyright © Harismita Vaideswaran 2025

10 9 8 7 6 5 4 3 2 1

P-ISBN: 9789353457846
E-ISBN: 9789353453381

The views and opinions expressed in this book are the author's own. The facts contained herein were reported to be true as on the date of publication by the author to the publishers of the book, and the publishers are not in any way liable for their accuracy or veracity.

All rights reserved. No part of this publication may be reproduced, transmitted or stored in a retrieval system in any form or by any means without the written permission of the publisher.

Typeset in Futura Std by R. Ajith Kumar, Noida

Printed at Thomson Press India Ltd

For Appa
*You've made me the writer I am today –
thank you for giving me the courage to do
what I love, and do it wholeheartedly.*

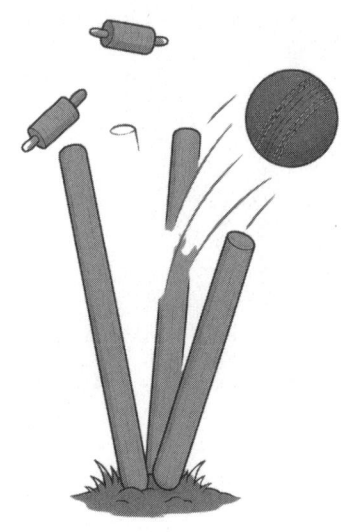

CONTENTS

1. Are We Champions?   1
2. Where It All Began   13
3. 'There Will Be Time for Cricket Later'   27
4. The Training Wheels Are Wobbling   41
5. It's Game Time   55
6. Welcome to the League of Giants   69
7. Reporting for Duty   83
8. The Cup of the World   95
9. We Are the Champions   109
10. Rohit Gurunath Sharma – The Man   117
11. Epilogue   127

1

ARE WE CHAMPIONS?

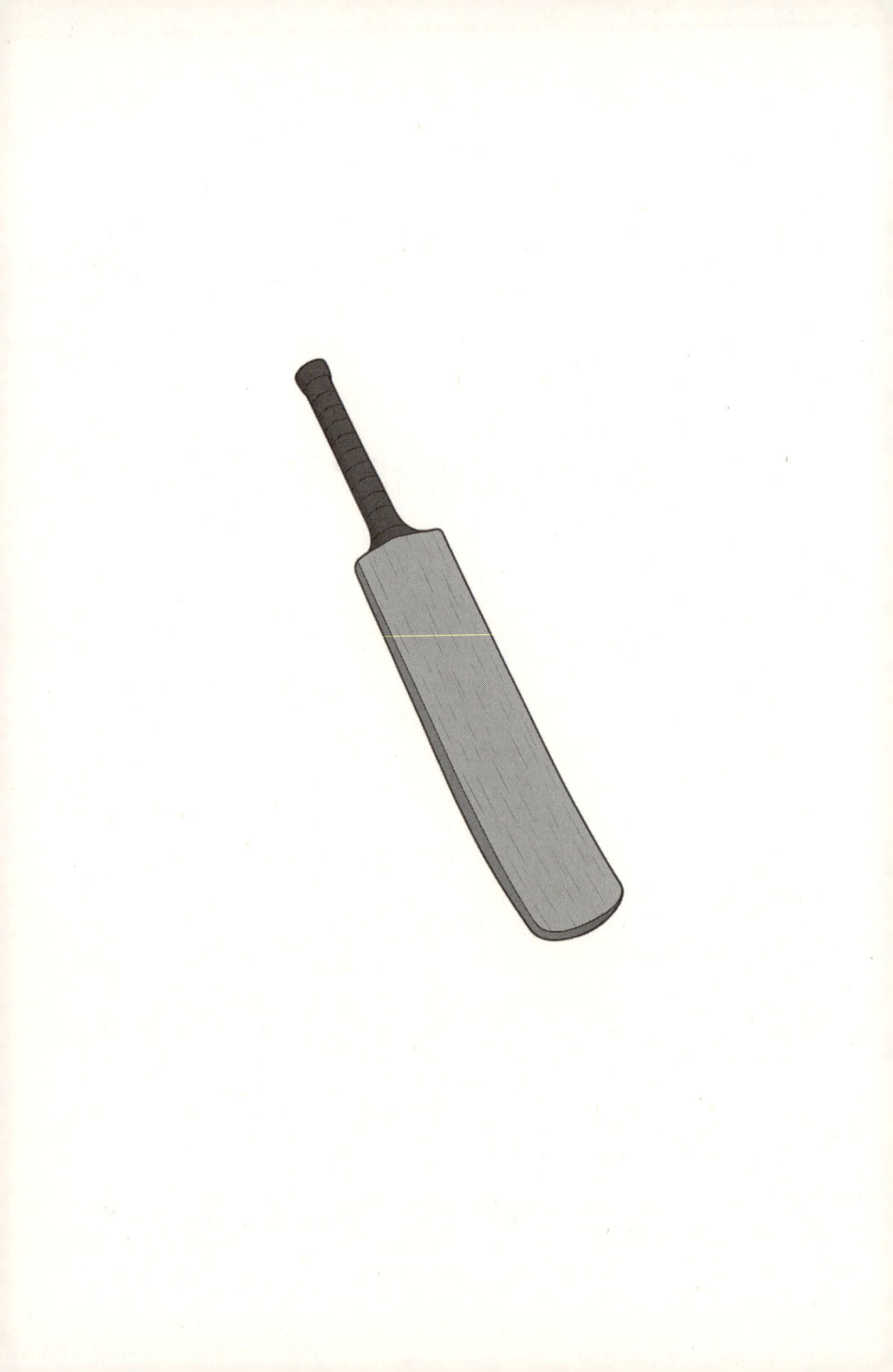

There is a deafening roar in the distance. If you were to stand on the field right now, the crowd's cheers would be all you hear. In the Indian cricket team's dressing room, though, there is silence. Players are strapping on pads. The batters are closing their eyes and breathing deeply, while others are discussing the first half of the match in hushed voices.

Rohit Sharma stands in a corner of the dressing room, leaning against a wall. He's holding his bat, tossing it from his left hand to his right and back again, staring into the distance. He does this over and over again, and if you looked at him right now, you would think he

was deep in thought, probably strategizing, his brows all furrowed.

His heart is racing in his chest, thumping loudly. Feeling the texture of the bat's grip helps him focus. What Rohit is really doing is trying to calm down, find his composure before the big innings.

A tall, young man walks towards him, holding his own bat like a spear. Rohit stills and looks up at him.

'Ready?' he asks Shubman Gill.

'Ready, Skip.' Shubman nods.

The two openers – the first batters to start the innings – jog to the pitch, warming up for what is to come. Shubman enters the field in a brisk jog, stretching his arms, brandishing his bat like a sword. Rohit walks slower, trailing a little. His face is all focus and concentration.

This is the Champions Trophy final, and it's all on the line for Captain Rohit Sharma.

Are We Champions?

You can't always predict how things will go when you get on the field to play cricket. No matter how much you practise and train, the game always has new ways of surprising you.

Some days, everything will feel just right. You will see the ball coming and know exactly how and when to hit it. You will send it flying to the boundary or slip it through a gap where there are no fielders. You feel like the game is made for you; the bowler bowls what you play best and the fielders never see you coming.

On other days, everything that can go wrong, does. The ball's too quick, or the bowler is smart and surprises you. Your bat feels strange in your hands, and you can't predict how the ball will come at you. The fielders are standing too close, and the wicketkeeper is just too quick. On days like this, you can't remember if you're any good at the game at all.

Rohit has played both kinds of games recently. This one, the Champions Trophy final, is a big one. India has finished bowling in the first innings, and it's time for the batters to fight for the win. The pressure is high, and much of it is on Rohit as the team's captain. It's like a final exam. You love the subject, but you know you have to do well. He can't afford to have a bad day today.

Rohit's mind is full of questions, and they are all directed at himself. *What if I get out too soon? What if the bowler is too quick, too good? We've lost to New Zealand before, what if we lose today? What if it's my fault? What if this is a bad day?* He is naturally nervous and scared. There is, after all, a lot on the line.

Rohit takes a deep breath as he reaches the stumps on the field and takes his place. As the captain of the other team arranges his fielders, Rohit remembers the good days. All the reasons he started playing cricket in the first place. How happy he used to feel playing cricket on the streets of Bombay with his friends. How every

ball made his heart sing. How his biggest dream was to wear India's bright blue jersey, just like his greatest heroes. How he wanted to make something of himself for his parents, his family, his country.

Rohit remembers what his uncle once told him all those years ago: 'Play bravely, Rohit.'

No matter how the match goes today, Rohit makes himself a promise. He will try his hardest, and win or lose, he will play to know that he has done his very best for his team, his country. He will play so he can hold his head high, no matter the result.

Captain Rohit Sharma, one of the greatest opening batsmen in cricket, takes his place in front of the wicket. He knocks the bat on the muddy brown pitch twice as the bowler runs at him, all fierce eyes.

Time to play.

> '*I had no idea how to come back [from losing the 2023 Cricket World Cup Final]. The first few days ... my family, my friends kept me going, kept things pretty light around me, which was quite helpful. It wasn't easy to digest, but yeah, life moves on. You have to move on in life. But honestly, it was tough. It was not so easy to just move on. I've always grown up watching 50-over World Cups and to me that was, you know, the ultimate prize: the 50-over World Cup.*'
>
> — ROHIT SHARMA

2
WHERE IT ALL BEGAN

Rohit Sharma was born on 30 April 1987 in a home in Nagpur that spoke a lot of languages. His mother, Purnima, came to Maharashtra from Visakhapatnam, Andhra Pradesh, and lived there with her husband, Gurunath, who took care of a warehouse for a transport company in Bombay. Rohit grew up listening to Telugu, his mother tongue, alongside Marathi – because he lived in Maharashtra – and, of course, English and Hindi.

Rohit did not live with his parents when he was a child. Bombay was an expensive city even in the eighties and nineties, and his father was the only one who worked in their family.

Instead, Rohit lived with his grandparents and uncles across the city.

Most of Rohit's days looked much like yours might have. He would go to school in the mornings, and when he came home, tired from a day full of studying, he would put his bag down and scarf down the lunch his grandmother had made for him. He would run through his homework as quickly as he could so that he could go play cricket with his younger brother, Vishal, and their friends.

His weekends were different from that of most of his classmates – he would go see his parents, taking the local train. Rohit found this very difficult when his family first moved from Nagpur to Bombay and he was sent to live with his uncles and grandparents in Dombivli, across the city from where his father worked. He wished he could live with his parents. He missed his mum's cooking, and spending time with his dad in the evenings. He was a brave

young boy though, and soon got used to the new order of things.

Rohit eventually came to enjoy the trips to see his parents, excitedly telling them about his week – what he learned in school, how well he had played in the neighbouring gully, the older kids he had bowled to, the wickets he had taken, the runs he had scored. Rohit loved bowling more than anything. If there was a match on TV, he would never miss it. He would sit in front of the TV with Vishal and they would watch India play, cheering whenever a ball went flying past the boundary, when a fielder leaped high and soared upwards to take a catch or when the stumps went flying with a rattle. He would watch the players dressed in the bright blue jerseys of Team India running around on the field, and he would dream of being one of them.

For all the joys of being a kid in his life – cricket, his friends, his grandparents, his uncles – he also knew all wasn't well at home. His father

was a hard-working man, and a deeply loyal one when it came to his job. He worked hard at the warehouse, but it was difficult to take care of a family of four with the money he made. They lived in a small room in the city, and money was often a struggle. Salaries would come late – the transport company was struggling – but his father never gave up on his work.

Rohit inherited this sense of responsibility and loyalty from his father. Though only twelve years old at the time, he felt like he should do something to help his father with taking care of the family. He would work hard at school and play even harder on the streets. He loved it, of course, and he was, more often than not, happy, but he also wanted to make something of himself.

When he watched matches on TV, he would imagine himself walking on to the field, bowling to the greats of the game, playing alongside the likes of Sachin Tendulkar. He would also

imagine allowing his father to rest, finally, and taking care of his mother. He would dream about living with his parents.

Rohit's favourite cricketer was Virender Sehwag, a fierce and explosive batter whenever he stepped up to the crease. He was known to bring even the most fearsome bowlers to their knees by battering their unplayable balls to the boundary lines. A destructive batter, they called him.

Rohit was in school when he heard that Sehwag had come to Mumbai to practice.

As he heard his classmates excitedly chatter away about where Sehwag was, a plan quietly took shape in Rohit's mind. When the bell rang at the end of lunchtime, Rohit quietly put his bag on his shoulders and slipped out of school while everyone was bustling away to class, laughing and jostling, waiting for the end of school.

He made it to the stadium, sweaty, still dressed in his school uniform, and walked in

like he belonged there. He ran to the fencing that separated the spectator area from where the players were training.

'Viru Paaji!' he shouted from the fence, giddy with excitement at seeing his idol – real and in the flesh – right before his eyes.

Sehwag turned around to look for a second, before focusing again on the net bowler coming at him. When he smacked the ball away for what would have been a boundary in a real match, everyone erupted in cheers and shouts of 'shot hai!'

Rohit stayed for the full training session, not wanting to miss a single moment of watching Viru Paaji bat.

When Sehwag walked up to leave, with his kitbag trailing behind him, Rohit was ready with a notebook he had pulled out of his bag to ask for an autograph. Sehwag smiled at him and signed it. Rohit watched him walk away, his heart beating wildly in his chest.

One day, Rohit Sharma would call that stadium his home, his home ground, and one day, he would share a dressing room and a cricket pitch with Sehwag, taking India to a great win. But he didn't know any of that yet.

> 'Who wouldn't miss a player like Rohit Sharma? Whether it's Test cricket, ODI cricket or T20 cricket, he always provided full entertainment. Fans enjoyed watching his batting, and the records he's made are outstanding.'
>
> — VIRENDER SEHWAG

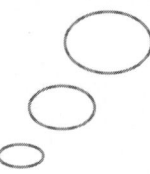

3

'THERE WILL BE TIME FOR CRICKET LATER'

> **ANNOUNCEMENT:**
>
> # CRICKET SUMMER CAMP
>
> Registration Fee: Rs 800
> Register in
> the school office at 3 p.m.
> Deadline: Next Friday

Rohit was standing at the noticeboard, surrounded by schoolmates, and everyone was pushing each other aside to look at the shiny, crisp new announcement that had appeared just this morning.

'Can you quit pushing!' he snapped at the boy next to him who had rammed his shoulder

'There Will Be Time for Cricket Later'

into Rohit's to get a better look at the sheet of paper. Rohit turned back to look at it, his brows furrowed. He made a mental note of the deadline – and the fee – before jostling his way out of the crowd.

Seeing Viru Paaji train on the field, watching matches at home, even playing on the streets, all of it was one thing. It was fun and exciting, but Rohit was twelve years old now, and serious about the game. He wanted to get good at cricket. *Really good*. Playing gully cricket just wasn't enough for him anymore.

The summer camp couldn't have come at a better time – or a worse one. Playing cricket meant that he would need money, and he didn't have any of his own. He couldn't ask his parents; things were difficult enough for them as it is. His family, too, was struggling, although things were easier here, with his uncles around. Rs 800, though – that was a big ask in the best of times, and these weren't the best of times.

Rohit was lost in thought all day. His maths teacher had to call his name thrice before he realized he was being asked to solve a problem on the blackboard. He tried to focus, but he couldn't stop thinking about the summer camp. He forgot to carry a number over and got the answer wrong, and when the class giggled and the teacher told him off for not paying attention, he barely noticed.

He went home in a sour mood. When his grandmother placed his favourite food – dal, rice and rasam – before him, he wasn't nearly as excited as he would normally be. He sat in front of his plate, pushing it around, eating unusually slowly.

His grandmother noticed, of course, as all grandmothers would. She nudged his shoulder gently. 'What's wrong? Why aren't you eating?'

Rohit shook his head, refusing to say anything.

Rohit's grandmother would not give up so easily. After all, what was a measly shake of the

head for a loving, affectionate and determined grandmother? Rohit's Ajji was all three, and it wasn't long before the answer was teased and cajoled out of the grumpy young man.

'Such a small problem, and you'll give up eating and go on a hunger strike, is it?' Ajji teased. 'Everyone needs help from time to time. If you need help, all you have to do is ask for it. But you must ask – and always with your head held high.'

She gave him a knowing pat on the head before clearing the table.

That evening, by the time his uncle came home from work, Rohit had worked out a plan and hashed out every detail in his mind. When dinner was done and the house had fallen into the easy silence of the night, Rohit worked up all his courage before walking up to his uncle and tapping him on his shoulder.

'Hmm?' he grunted.

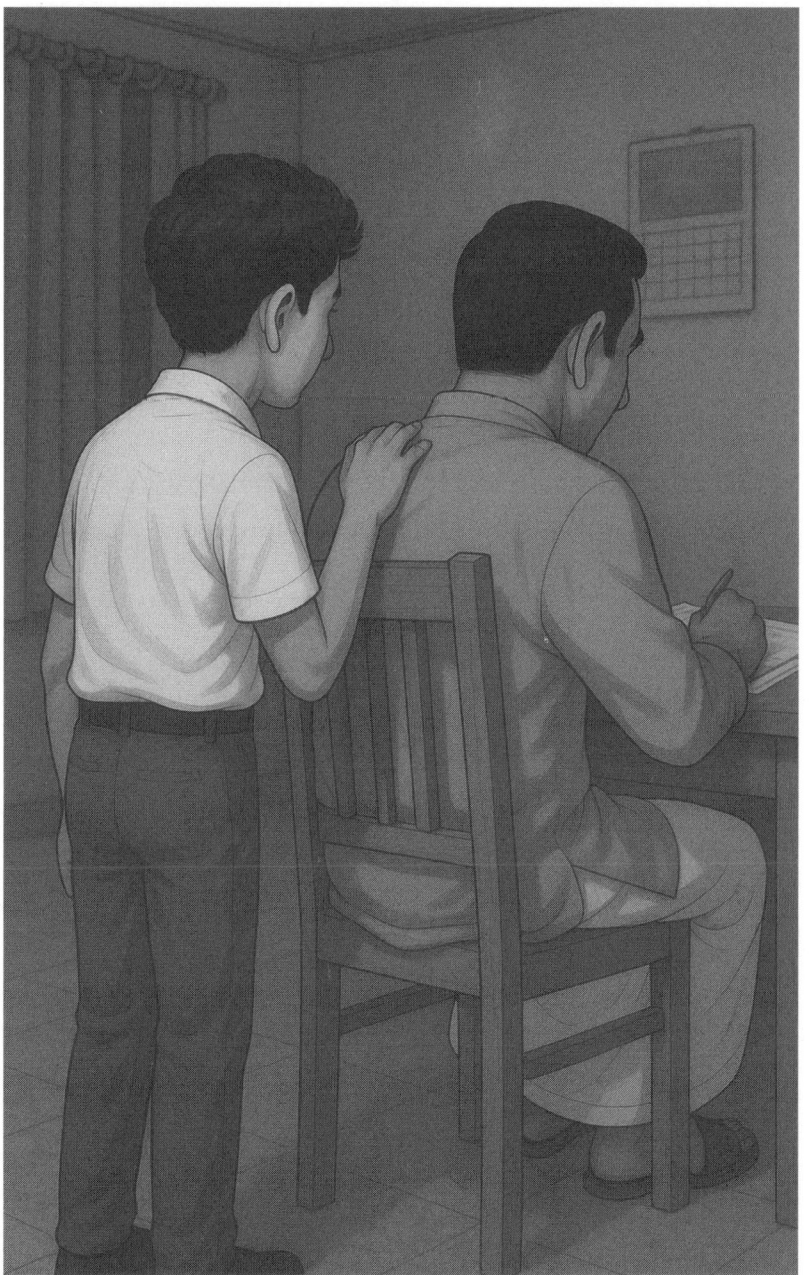

'Kaka there's a summer camp for cricket and it costs 800 rupees can I have some money to register?'

Rohit didn't mean for this to happen, but when he saw his uncle's face, the plan went flying out of the window, and his words came tumbling out of his mouth like he had no control.

His uncle looked at him, utterly befuddled, having understood absolutely nothing of what the boy had just said.

'Start again – go slower this time, beta, I didn't catch a word of that.'

Deep breath. He took one, and, suddenly remembering what Ajji had said earlier, stood a little straighter, looked up at his uncle, head held high, and tried again.

'Kaka, there's a cricket summer camp. It costs Rs 800 and I want to go. Can I please have some money to register?'

Kaka looked at him with a kind smile and slightly sad eyes. 'That's a lot of money, Rohit.

Besides, I think you should focus on working hard in school and studying for your exams. This is an important time.'

'I want to play cricket, Kaka, and I think I would be good at it.' He allowed a little bit of his pride and confidence to seep into his voice.

'Studies first – all this later. There will be plenty of time to play after you do well in school.' Kaka's voice was definitive.

Rohit wasn't one to give up, though, and what Ajji had said earlier in the day stuck with him. If you need help, you'll have to ask – with your head held high.

That's just what Rohit did. Calmly, gently, but always firmly and confidently, he asked his Kaka the same thing every day: He wanted to join the cricket summer camp, and he needed money for it. He never raised his voice, never cried, never threw any tantrums.

When his Kaka noticed how hard he was studying – and how much harder he was playing – he relented. He handed him two Rs 100 notes: 'You are a persistent young man. Here, this is all I can give you.'

As Rohit walked away, the notes clutched in his hand – it wasn't all he needed, but it was something – his uncle called after him: 'Play bravely, Rohit.'

This too would stick with him, from the moment he joined that cricket camp – it wasn't enough money, but Rohit was enough of a player, and then some – all the way till today.

> *In some 100-odd square feet house, we used to stay, eight of us ... six chachas, uncles and two aunts ... I have seen those days so I know nothing in life comes easy, I have to work hard. Whatever I am today is because of the hardship I have gone through. When you get things easily, you don't understand their importance. The way I grew up, I think, was a great help. I had to make every opportunity count because my past was always on my mind. I know what I had gone through, and didn't want to be in the same place again.'*
>
> — ROHIT SHARMA

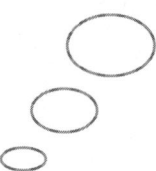

4

THE TRAINING WHEELS ARE WOBBLING

Dinesh Lad was a formidable-looking man when you first laid eyes on him. He sported a bushy moustache and was often to be found on the sidelines of the cricket field, wearing a cap, squinting in the sun at some young player or another. You might look at him and think he was displeased, but more often than not, he was just concentrating on the players in front of him, making note of their form, how they moved, how they played under pressure, how they talked to their teammates. Lad had a sharp eye for promising cricketing talent – he was the head coach of cricket at the Vivekanand High

School in Mumbai, a school that was known for its cricketing facilities.

That summer, he wasn't at school, though – he had a cricket summer camp to coach. At that very moment, he was squinting at the young off-spin bowler whose face was scrunched up in concentration as he took his run-up.

From where Lad was standing, the batter never stood a chance. The ball spun away easily from him and struck the stumps with a satisfying rattle, sending the bails flying. The bowler stuck his hand up, one finger pointing to the sky, appealing the wicket. The umpire's verdict was swift – that was a wicket.

Adjusting his cap, Lad called: 'Rohit! Come here.'

Rohit looked up from his team huddle, a little startled, before jogging up to the coach. He hadn't bowled a no-ball, and he thought that had been a good delivery. What was this

about? Coach never called on the players while they were in the middle of a match.

'Yes, sir!' he called as he came to a stop in front of the coach.

'Good delivery.' Lad nodded. 'Tell me, Rohit, which school do you study in?'

Still unsure of where this conversation was headed, Rohit answered: 'Our Lady of Vailankanni High School, sir.'

'You should consider taking admission in Vivekanand next year. They have much better cricketing facilities – you'd do well there.'

Rohit knew about the school; he also knew his family probably couldn't afford its fees.

Ask for help when you need it – ask with your head held high.

He hesitated for a moment before replying: 'Thank you, sir, I know of the school. I also know you coach there. I can't afford to go there. I mean, my family can't.'

Lad's eyes softened a little. 'All right, back to the match. We'll speak later.'

That day, Lad made his way to his school lost in thought. Rohit was certainly a promising young man. He played with focus, and the kind of zeal and determination he rarely saw in boys of this age. Rohit also had a sharp mind for the game – he set the field expertly, almost like he knew exactly what the batter would do with his delivery. Almost like he could see exactly what would happen.

Lad didn't go to his office as he normally would; instead, he headed straight to the principal's office. Lad was never a man to beat around the bush.

'There's this kid at the summer camp. His name is Rohit Gurunath Sharma, and he's an exceptionally promising cricketer. He's a menace on the field when he takes the ball in his hand, and as a coach, he's a joy to watch. I'd like to offer him a scholarship for our school. What can we do?'

The talks were long, and often arduous. There was a lot of talk of numbers, and it took days to have things settled. Finally, a decision was reached.

'You can tell him tomorrow,' the principal said with a smile.

Rohit was warming up on the field with a jog when Lad called out his name again. 'Come here – I need a word.'

Rohit turned his path towards Lad, but he didn't stop jogging.

'Yes, sir?' Rohit couldn't keep the inquiry out of his voice this time.

'There's a scholarship waiting for you at Vivekanand High School. You don't have to pay a penny. Join the school – and I want to see you on the field.'

'Yes, sir.' Rohit hesitated. 'Thank you, sir.' He held out his hand, offering a handshake. It was the grown-up thing to do, after all.

Lad smiled at him and patted his shoulder before shaking his hand. 'Go, finish your warm-up. See you in school.'

Rohit didn't walk home from the bus that evening. He sprinted to tell his grandmother and grandfather the news. Then his uncle, when he got back from work. They were thrilled, of course, but there were all the logistics of a school transfer to think about. He went to bed that night thinking about how he'd tell his parents over the weekend.

A few months later, Rohit would join his new school, and walk on to the field to play cricket on the new grounds. He would be coached by Dinesh Lad. One day, the whole world would know his name – but not as a bowler.

> *'Rohit used to practise with a wet tennis ball; it would skid down the lane. The way Rohit plays straight shots and then pull shots, I think it was his practice with a tennis ball that helped him better his shots.'*
>
> — DINESH LAD

5
IT'S GAME TIME

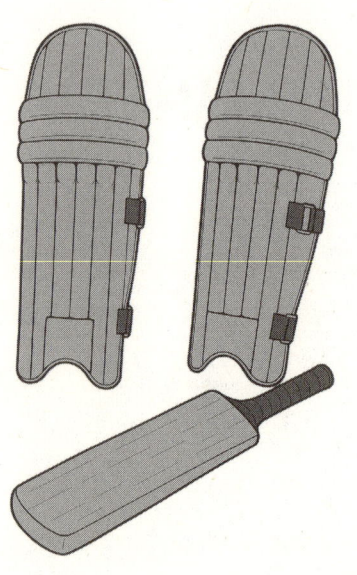

It was no surprise to anyone, least of all Lad, that Rohit did spectacularly in the Mumbai cricket circuit. Lad noticed that while Rohit had begun as a bowler, his true prowess lay in batting. He was aggressive, calculating, and more often than not knew how – and when – to knock it out of the park. Rohit trained hard at school, and while studying had its place in his life – as it must at that age – his mind and body both belonged to cricket. The hours were long, but he never stopped working hard – and having fun! – on the field. He made fast friends with his classmates and teammates, and was well-liked by almost everyone. Being an excellent

cricketer certainly helped with making new friends. Rohit became very popular because he was funny, and always up for a conversation about anything under the sun.

Rohit had no trouble being selected for his school team for the Harris and Giles Shield tournaments in Mumbai. The Harris Shield was a tournament for young cricketers of Mumbai under sixteen years old, and the Giles Shield was for even younger players, those who were under fourteen years old. The tournament took place among the schools of the city, and it was a matter of great prestige for the boys who got to play. As all the young – and serious – cricketers of Rohit's age knew, this was also where the Mumbai Cricket Association's selectors looked for fresh young talent to play for the state.

While the tournaments were challenging, Rohit did well in them. It didn't take a lot of time for people to sit up and take notice of his natural instincts for cricket – and all the hard work he put into sharpening those instincts to be lethal on the field. He was swiftly snapped up by the under-fourteen Mumbai team, with whom he began to represent his state against other state teams from all over India.

Rohit rose through the ranks of domestic cricket very quickly, garnering the attention of sharp-eyed selectors, who marked him down as one to watch. His first big moment on the international stage came at the under-nineteen World Cup in 2006, where he played alongside other would-be greats of the game like Ravindra Jadeja, Cheteshwar Pujara and Piyush Chawla. He won Player of the Match for an excellent batting performance – called a knock in cricket – against Sri Lanka by scoring 78 runs in 105 balls, a great score in a one-day match, which is played for 50 overs by each team. He also took a wicket, letting the batting side take only 3 runs while he bowled.

This was a List A match, though – for young cricketers – and his true debut for Team India came later, when he was twenty years old. By the time 2007 rolled around, Rohit had graduated from school and started college. He was also doing very well in domestic cricket, and after a lot of thinking, he decided he wanted to focus on cricket. When Rohit got his first call-up to wear the bright blue India jersey he had dreamed of for as long as he could remember, he had left college and dedicated all his time to the sport he loved so much. He was ready to take on the responsibility of his family and take care of his parents, and he didn't want to waste any time on distractions.

It was the end of May in 2007 when Rohit received the call. The selectors had been watching him keenly in domestic tournaments, and he had proved himself time and time again, be it in the Deodhar Trophy, the Duleep Trophy or the legendary Ranji Trophy. They liked what

they saw, they said, and they wanted him to fly to Belfast, Northern Ireland, as part of Team India's squad. Thus, Rohit donned Team India's blue jersey for the first time in Ireland, far away from home, and became part of India's legendary cricket team.

It was an easy match for India. The opposing Irish team had racked up a low total, and Rohit didn't even need to step up before the early batters made the score the team needed to win.

Rohit never forgot that day, though, and he never forgot or lost sight of the pride he felt when he first put that jersey on.

The years to come would not prove easy for Rohit. He was a talented player – that was clear to everyone who saw him play – but he was not always consistent, nor always reliable on the field. He was prone to having some phenomenal days on the field followed by many bad days. Days when he would miscalculate and send the ball straight into the fielder's hand. Days when

the ball would spin the wrong way and hit the stumps before he could react.

The selectors saw his potential, but they also made note of this. He would have to work very hard indeed to prove himself worthy of staying in the team consistently. Worthy of stepping up to the crease and getting to play for India.

> *'No matter how talented you are or naturally gifted you are, there's no substitute to hard work if you got to maintain standards.'*
> — ROHIT SHARMA

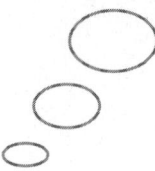

Fun Fact

Cricket is played in three formats: Test cricket, the oldest, most prestigious form in which one match takes place over five days; one-day cricket, which is played for the full day, and each side gets 50 overs to bat; and T20 cricket, the youngest format, where each side gets 20 overs to bat.

International Test series take place between countries in sets of three to five matches, and some of the most famous Test series are the Border–Gavaskar Trophy played between India and Australia, and the Ashes series, played between Australia and England. The prestigious Ranji Trophy in Indian domestic cricket is a domestic first-class (also called days cricket) tournament.

The International Cricket Council (ICC) Cricket World Cup and the Asian Cricket Council (ACC) Asia Cup are both 50-over tournaments, while the ICC T20 World Cup and the Indian Premier League are played in the T20 format.

6

WELCOME TO THE LEAGUE OF GIANTS

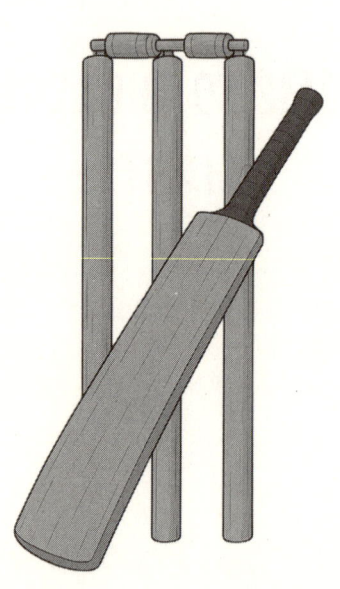

FORTHCOMING ATTRACTION
27 FEBRUARY 2008

Watch Sharma play his trademark fluent covervdrives or square-drives of the back foot and you get the impression of a top-quality cricketer. Much of it has to do with the effortlessness with which he can get his wrists and body into a position from where he can direct the ball to where he wants, and do it with time to spare – a quality only the great or the very good possess.

The year 2008 was a highlight year for Rohit. He had been playing international cricket for just two years – slightly over twenty-four matches – but he had made his mark as a force to be reckoned with.

He was being touted as the replacement for Sachin Tendulkar's number four spot in the team. Mahendra Singh Dhoni saw him as a trusted partner on the crease. When the first-ever Indian Premier League auctions took place in 2008, Rohit was snapped up by the Deccan Chargers for Rs 4.8 crore.

All that he had set out to do as a young boy – give his family security, a comfortable life – he had already accomplished at the age of twenty. When his brother, Vishal, wanted to go abroad to study in Florida, America, Rohit stepped up and confidently said he would go; money would be no trouble. His parents, Purnima and Gurunath Sharma, were happy and comfortable – local

celebrities, in fact – where they now lived. In 2007, in an India vs Pakistan match – one of the greatest cricketing rivalries in the world – Rohit batted alongside a legendary opener in Gwalior. A batter he had admired for as long as he could remember. He scored the first one-day half-century of his career with Virender Sehwag by his side.

Six years later, well into his international career, having debuted in all three formats – T20, one-day and Test – he would make history by creating a record that still stands to this day.

The year was 2014. It was November in Kolkata. Hot, humid, but not unpleasantly so. Sri Lanka was touring India, and their next match was to take place in the legendary Eden Gardens. Rohit Sharma was slated to open with Ajinkya Rahane, and the Indian team, captained by none other than Virat Kohli himself, had the likes of Suresh Raina and the young gun Axar Patel on the roster. It was going to be a thriller

of a match, and the whole country was holding its breath. On the morning of 13 November 2014, nobody knew history was going to be made at Eden Gardens.

Rohit took a deep breath before he began the jog up to the crease. The openers took their places, and Rohit took one last look at the cheering stands before tuning it all out to focus on the action in front of him. They got off to a strong start. Rahane and Rohit found an easy rhythm in their partnership. The match was just short of 8 overs in when a ball struck Rahane on the pads. The umpire ruled him out, the wicket taken. His legs had been directly in line with the stumps, and had his leg not stopped the ball, he would have been bowled out. This was an LBW wicket, and Rahane was out of the game.

For Rohit, however, this was a good cricketing day. The weather was perfect. The crowds cheers seemed to act as fuel, swirling around him, pushing him to focus even better. The

bowlers seemed to be bowling just for him. He seemed to instinctively know where to aim for the ball; the bat felt like a perfect extension of his hand. When Rohit found his rhythm that day, he was a force to be reckoned with. Batters came and went; bowlers came and went. Rohit stayed, and Rohit *played*, smashing the ball to the boundary every chance he got.

Another couple of overs in, Virat Kohli stepped up with the bat in hand. Rohit and Virat met at the middle of the two stumps to bump fists, and Rohit gave him a quick rundown of how the ball was behaving on the pitch. When Rohit found his rhythm, he was brilliant; when Rohit and Virat – Ro-Ko, as they are affectionately called by fans – partnered on the crease, they were unstoppable. Virat scored 66 runs before a miscalculation while taking a run led to him being run-out.

That day belonged to Rohit in every way. He hit a total of 33 fours and 9 sixes, and batted

with five batters of his own team before an expertly bowled delivery – four balls before the end of the innings by Nuwan Kulasekara, a dangerously good Sri Lankan fast bowler – led to Rohit being caught out by Mahela Jayawardene.

India had racked up a spectacular total of over 400 runs and battered Sri Lanka in the process, sweeping the win by 153 runs.

Rohit scored 264 of those runs single-handedly that day.

Even today, this is the most runs anyone has ever been able to score in a 50-over innings in the history of the game.

> *'Nothing is easy in cricket. Maybe when you watch it on TV, it looks easy. But it is not. You have to use your brain and time the ball.'*
>
> — ROHIT SHARMA

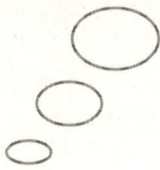

7
REPORTING FOR DUTY

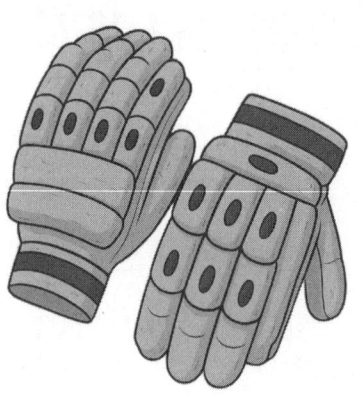

The decade of the 2010s saw the rise of a new generation of young blood in Indian cricket. Virat Kohli had taken over as captain in all formats of the game in 2017; M.S. Dhoni had retired from international cricket. Virat was fierce, aggressive and kind of scary when he got all focused on the field. Although Rohit was Virat's senior in terms of both birthday age and cricketing age, Virat was more consistent. When Virat needed a break, Rohit would step up to be captain, often swapping the position with K.L. Rahul, a deliberate, calm batter, and Ajinkya Rahane.

In 2018, the Asia Cup – the biggest international 50-over tournament after ICC's – was taking place and Virat wasn't around to be captain. Rohit stepped in, and India swept the championship with a decisive victory that surprised everyone. India didn't have an exceptionally strong team that year, and were under a lot of pressure, but it turned out the young boy from Mumbai had grown up to be a level-headed captain who was very good at leading under pressure. The whole world took notice of this win, and who led India to it, including the organization that manages cricket in India, the Board of Control for Cricket in India, the BCCI.

In 2021, when Virat decided he wanted to step down from his captaincy so he could focus on his work and family better, Rohit was the natural choice for the BCCI. He became the T20 captain first, and then the One Day International (ODI) captain. A few months later, after a particularly bad series losses for India versus South Africa, Kohli stepped down from the throne of captain, and it was passed on to Rohit Gurunath Sharma.

By this time, Rohit had proved himself time and time again. He had won the Indian Premier League championship title six times – still the most any individual player has won; once with the team that originally swooped in on him, the Deccan Chargers, and five times with one of the most successful teams in the tournament, the Mumbai Indians, for whom he still plays.

The team loved Rohit as captain. Bowlers loved him, young batters looked up to him with admiration and asked him for advice in the dressing room, which he was always more than happy to offer. Everyone loved playing under him. He was smart, with a canny understanding of how batters thought and how bowlers bowled. He was great at setting smart fields so his team would be prepared to catch what the opposition's batters hit.

He had also acquired a reputation for being a captain who listened closely and listened well to what his team was telling him. His particular way of setting the field and using his bowlers effectively was quickly becoming the stuff of legend. He also had excellent coaches to guide his way. He had begun to step in as captain under the legendary Ravi Shastri, and had then captained the team under the greats of the game like Rahul Dravid and Gautam Gambhir.

Rohit was also very chilled out on the field. He kept his cool, and often joked with players, especially when he had to tell them off for carelessness. If they were bowling badly, he was quick to correct them with a sharp joke. If his fielders weren't paying enough attention, he'd tell them to stop acting like they were walking in a garden. If the bowler was bowling the wrong length, Rohit would notice, and tell the bowler

exactly how the ball would behave if he just listened to him.

He often fielded in the slips, right by the wicket-keeper, so he could keep an eye on the full team and the opposing batters. He ran a tight ship as captain, but it was also a successful one.

Besides being a great captain, Rohit was still a menace for the opposing team when he stepped up to the field. His nickname, Hitman, had been cemented in the language of the game, and he proved it nearly every time he stepped up to the crease.

When Rohit retired from the T20 format in 2024, the whole country hailed it as the end of an era in Indian cricket. Rohit would come to be known as one of India's most successful captains in the format, and one of the best opening batters of all time.

> *'The real challenge is not to face the world outside, but to take the first step in challenging yourself.'*
>
> — ROHIT SHARMA

8
THE CUP OF THE WORLD

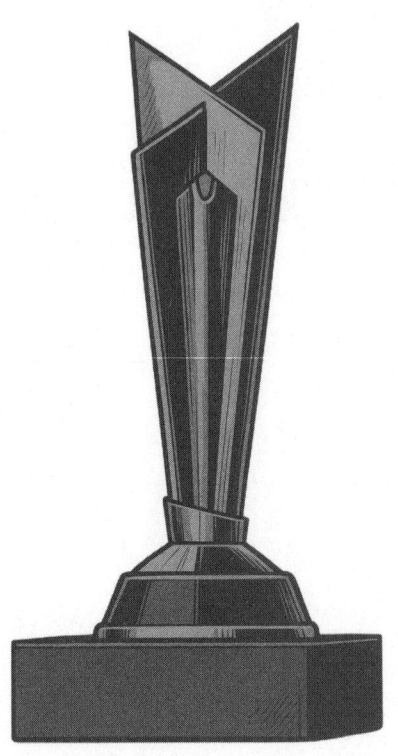

JANUARY 2011, BANGALORE

There's a slight nip in the air in January in Bangalore. The weather is pleasant, and the city has an easy rhythm to the way it moves. For Rohit, though, this is a time of anticipation – he is nervous, eager, scared. India is hosting the ICC Cricket World Cup, the international holy grail of one-day cricket, in a couple of months, and Rohit is training in Bangalore.

Every young cricketer has only one goal that year: to be included in the team list. Mahendra Singh Dhoni is captain, and the vice captain is

Rohit's hero, Sehwag. When calls for the squad go out and BCCI releases the squad list, there is no Rohit Sharma on it. Rohit is devastated when he doesn't see his name.

He sees his friends on the list: Piyush Chawla, the sharp spinner from Uttar Pradesh;

The Cup of the World

Ravichandran Ashwin, the canny, scientific Tamil Nadu player who shoots carrom ball-like bullets; Virat Kohli, the fiery young batter from Delhi. They would all be playing alongside legends of the game: Sachin Tendulkar, Dhoni, Sehwag. The final would be taking place in Wankhede Stadium in Mumbai. *At home.*

Rohit is devastated. He walks out, alone, and sits on the grass, trying hard to hold back his tears. His chest feels tight, his hands are clutched into fists. *How did this happen?*

Deep in his heart, Rohit knows why. He hasn't been very consistent recently. One good day followed by three bad days will just not cut it if you want to play the big games. He would have to become someone nobody would even think about turning down for a spot on the squad. That year, Rohit refuses to watch any of the matches. His resolve crumbles later, when India makes it to the semi-final, and then the final, and he

India T20 World Cup, Squad List

Rohit Sharma (C)
Hardik Pandya
Yashasvi Jaiswal
Virat Kohli
Suryakumar Yadav
Rishabh Pant
Sanju Samson
Shivam Dube
Ravindra Jadeja
Axar Patel
Kuldeep Yadav
Yuzvendra Chahal
Arshdeep Singh
Jasprit Bumrah
Mohd Siraj

watches the final stages of the tournament. In that moment, he can only think about how he can run from how much this hurts.

India wins the ICC World Cup that year. For Rohit, it is the wake-up call he needs. He throws himself into training with discipline like a man possessed. When India lifts the cup, he truly believes deep down that he should have been there in the dugout. He promises himself he will not let this happen again. He will train harder, be better, be *braver*.

By 2013, two years later, he would become one of the most reliable openers in the Indian cricket team.

MAY 2024, MUMBAI

By the age of thirty-seven, Rohit has scored the most centuries in the T20 format. There is no question of whether he will be part of the squad; he's making the selections – he'll be captaining

The Cup of the World

the team. He doesn't know it at the time, but Rohit is about to ink history with his captaincy in what would be his final year in the international format of T20 cricket.

India makes it to the final of the tournament undefeated. The team is untouchable. The final in Barbados, though, is off to a rough start for the batting side. Rohit Sharma is out early, as are two of the other strong batters. When Virat Kohli steps up, they seem to find their footing again. The match is *very* close, though, and nobody really knows what will happen.

Rohit's mind comes through in the second innings, when India is bowling. He has a menacing set of bowlers by his side: the all-rounder Hardik Pandya and the brilliant fast bowler Jasprit Bumrah. Rohit has set the field well, and Suryakumar Yadav's flying catch over the boundary line would seal India's fate – although none of them know it at the time.

When Hardik Pandya bowls the last ball of the match, the stadium erupts in a deafening roar. He falls to his knees. India has won.

Rohit stands in the dressing room, but he can't seem to find his balance. His knees feel weak, like they'll give out at any moment, and his hands will not stop shaking. He isn't sure anything has really registered until he walks out of the dressing room, wobbling a little, and sees Virat walking up the stairs towards him. When they hug, almost stumbling into each other, victors and champions all, it really sinks in. The rest of the team has already rushed on to the field. Rohit and Virat are holding each other, laughing and crying all at once. There are tears. There is laughter. There is victory.

Under Rohit Sharma's sharp, brilliant style of captaincy, India brings home an ICC trophy for the first time in eleven years, since their last Champions Trophy win in 2013, under M.S. Dhoni. India has won the 2024 T20 World Cup

undefeated – the first in the history of the format and the tournament to pull it off.

After the victory lap was taken and the trophy was lifted, Rohit steps up alongside Virat and Ravindra Jadeja, and all three of them announce their retirement from playing T20 internationals. It is a farewell truly fit for a king. No. It is a farewell truly fit for the Hitman of Indian cricket.

> *'Everything takes time. You should not give up on yourself, you must continue with the courage to achieve success.'*
>
> — ROHIT SHARMA

9

WE ARE THE CHAMPIONS

9 MARCH 2025, DUBAI

Rohit has had more bad days than good ones recently. The series loss in Australia was terrible, and his Champions Trophy run so far has been a mixed bag. Dropped catches, awful knocks where he's out on a duck, having made no runs. Rumours of his retirement are swirling in the air. His form has been criticized, analysed and dissected over and over. Rohit is determined, though. This is a big one, and he's going to make it count.

And make it count he does.

Rohit finds his rhythm in the Champions Trophy final against New Zealand. He may be nervous, and the stakes may be higher than ever, but when Rohit finds his sense of balance on the crease, he is unstoppable. He makes a total of 76 runs before a tricky ball by the young Rachin Ravindra allows Tom Latham, New Zealand's quick wicket-keeper, to stump him out.

The world calls the knock 'classic Hitman' and 'vintage Rohit Sharma'. When India race to the victory by 4 wickets, the country erupts into screaming cheers for their hero again.

Under Rohit Gurunath Sharma, India brings home an ICC championship title for the seventh time. It's Rohit's second, the most an Indian captain has ever accomplished after Dhoni. Again and again, Rohit Sharma makes history by playing with all his heart, with all his bravery, with all the love in the world for the game that has made him who he is, and given him all that he has.

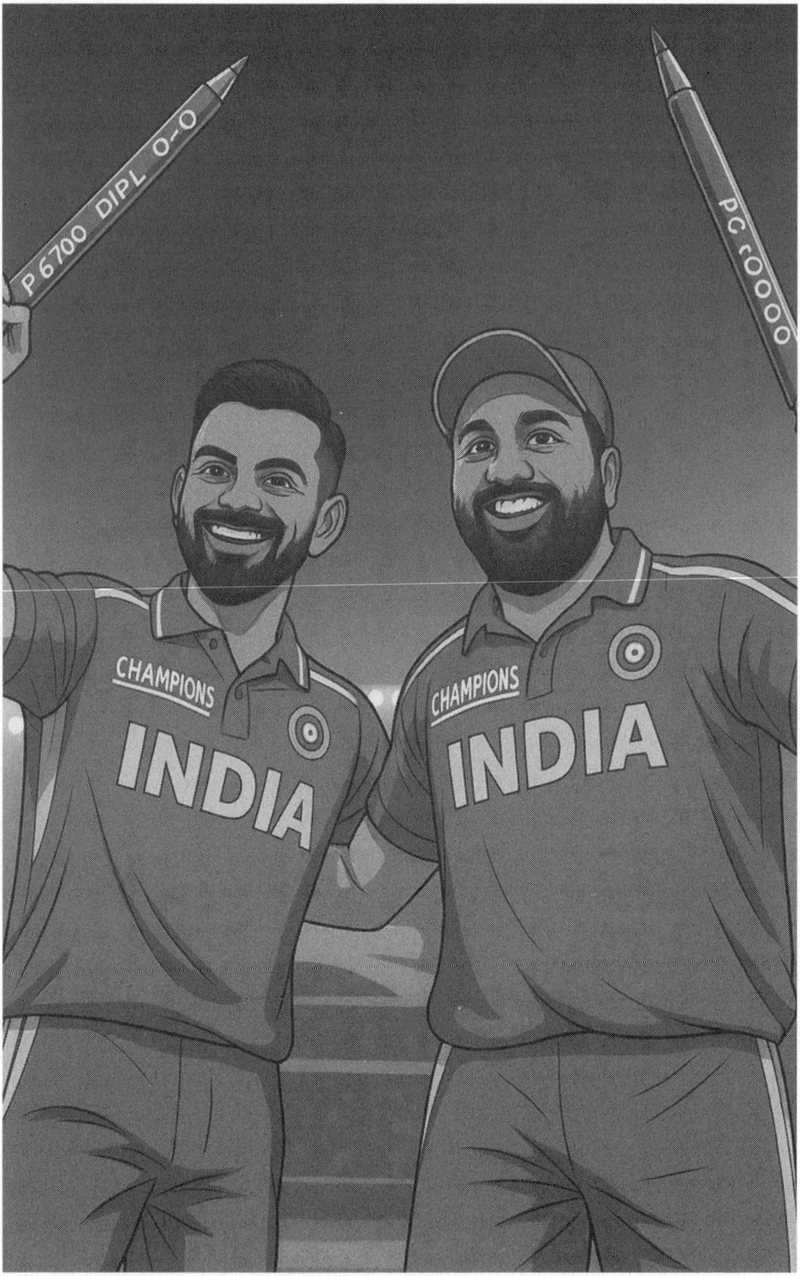
P 6700 DIPL O-O
PC cOOOO
CHAMPIONS
INDIA
CHAMPIONS
INDIA

We Are the Champions

As Virat and Rohit uproot the stumps from the pitch and perform a victory dance with each other to the endless joy of 1.4 billion Indians the world over, Rohit shouts gleefully, all laughter and bright, scrunched-up eyes: 'Let them say whatever they want. Like hell we're retiring!'

> 'Individual brilliance wins a few games, unity wins championships.'
>
> — ROHIT SHARMA

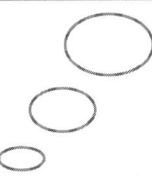

10

ROHIT GURUNATH SHARMA – THE MAN

Rohit lives with his wife, Ritika, and two kids, Samaira and Ahaan, in Mumbai.

He is mostly vegetarian, although he eats eggs, and loves Indian food more than anything else, even when he is travelling abroad for games. His favourite foods are dal-rice, rasam-rice, eggs and biryani.

Rohit has a big heart, and has been actively involved in charitable and philanthropic activities with organizations who work for the welfare of animals. He has worked with the Kenya government to save wild animals, and has even travelled to Nairobi to see the last northern white rhino in the world. He was so moved when he saw the last of the species in Kenya, and so deeply saddened when he died, that he returned to India and took a pledge to help save rhinos.

> *'My love for rhinos sparked when I first heard about Sudan, the last male northern white African rhino who passed away this year thus leading to the inevitable extinction of the entire species and that broke my heart. As the world and I mourned for my fallen friend Sudan, I researched the best way for me to help prevent something like this happening and the best way I know how is to create awareness.'*

Today, he works with the World Wildlife Fund in India to raise awareness on how to help and save rhinos.

He loves photography and nature, and watches a lot of documentaries about wildlife to relax. He's particularly fond of cheetahs.

When he's at home, Rohit loves hanging out with his kids, watching cartoons, and playing with his dog.

His favourite music is Punjabi and Bollywood music.

He is known to the world as the sleepyhead of his team – and Virat has mentioned how Rohit can sleep anywhere – on team buses, in the dressing room on practice days. If you can think of a place, Rohit's probably caught a nap in it.

> 'There are things we control – but things that are not in control, no point wasting time and energy on that.'
>
> – ROHIT SHARMA

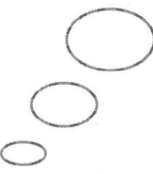

11
EPILOGUE

HINDUSTAN TIMES

> Rohit Sharma to get his own stand at Wankhede Stadium; to join legends Sunil Gavaskar and Sachin Tendulkar

When India itself was slowly growing and becoming better at cricket day by day, a young boy who lived in Mumbai had a dream. He wanted to play for India. He wanted to wear the cap of his country, don the bright blue jersey of one of the greatest cricket teams in the world.

He would look at Wankhede Stadium from afar, dreaming of playing there one day. Fifteen years later, he would call the stadium his home.

Thirty years later, the stadium would call him its own, claim him as belonging to its soil and grass – a legend of the game in his own right.

This is the kingdom of cricket – and Rohit Gurunath Sharma reigns over it as one of the greatest opening batters the game has ever seen, and one of the most successful captains India has ever had leading its side.

> 'You cannot have a perfect game. You can have a near-perfect game but never a perfect game.'
> — ROHIT SHARMA

ROHIT SHARMA: THE FACT FILE

ROHIT SHARMA'S BAT

Rohit Sharma uses a CEAT bat that is known for its thick edges, large sweet spot and slightly rounded face. These features are specially designed for his aggressive and precise style of batting.

Throughout his career, Rohit has switched between several notable cricket bat sponsors, including MRF (used famously by Virat Kohli), Reebok, Sunridges and Adidas. Since 2015, Rohit has been using CEAT-labelled bats.

After the famous Kanpur Test in Bangladesh in October 2024, Rohit received a bat from Bangladesh's Mehidy Hasan Miraz, who owns his own bat company called MKS Sports, in recognition of his excellence as a player.

THE WIN RECORD

Rohit Sharma was captain of the Indian cricket team from 2017 (temporarily) to 2025. He captained India in 142 matches and won 103 of them. He has won 72.53 per cent of the matches he has captained!

THE HIGHLIGHT REEL: TOP FIVE CAREER MOMENTS

1. **177 on Test debut: 2013 vs West Indies**
   In his very first Test match, Rohit Sharma made a spectacular mark at Eden Gardens with 177 runs. This is the second-highest debut score ever made by an Indian!

2. **264 in an ODI: 2014 vs Sri Lanka**
   At Eden Gardens again, Rohit made the record for the highest ODI score ever – a record still held by him, which you read about earlier in the book.

3. **Five centuries: 2019 ICC World Cup**

   In the 2019 ICC ODI World Cup, Rohit became the first-ever player to hit five centuries in a single tournament.

4. **ICC T20 World Cup, 2024**

   Captain Rohit Sharma led India to the ICC T20 World Cup in the final against South Africa – by just 7 runs! – and brought an ICC trophy home to India after a long, long wait.

5. **South Africa Tour of India, 2019 series**

   In 2019, Rohit was part of a change in the batting order in Tests: He became an opener. One of his best matches was the first Test against South Africa, where he scored back-to-back hundreds across two innings in Visakhapatnam. In the third Test of the same series in Ranchi, he scored a double century – 212 runs! This series made him a force to be reckoned with as an opener in the Test format.

LET'S TALK MILESTONES

Some very cool milestones Rohit Sharma has achieved in his career include scoring a century on his Test debut (177 runs) and a century across both innings of a Test match (against South Africa in Visakhapatnam in 2019).

In the ODI format, he has the impressive achievement of having taken 50 catches – also called fielding dismissals – and scoring 5,000 runs in the format.

TEST FORMAT

- **67** MATCHES
- **57.05** STRIKE RATE
- **116** INNINGS
- **12** CENTURIES
- **10** NOT OUTS
- **18** HALF-CENTURIES
- **4301** RUNS
- **88** SIXES
- **212** HIGHEST SCORE
- **473** FOURS
- **40.57** AVERAGE SCORE
- **68** CATCHES

ODI FORMAT

273 MATCHES	**92.8** STRIKE RATE
265 INNINGS	**32** CENTURIES
36 NOT OUTS	**58** HALF-CENTURIES
11168 RUNS	**344** SIXES
264 HIGHEST SCORE	**1045** FOURS
48.76 AVERAGE SCORE	**97** CATCHES

T20I FORMAT

- **159** MATCHES
- **140.89** STRIKE RATE
- **151** INNINGS
- **5** CENTURIES
- **19** NOT OUTS
- **32** HALF-CENTURIES
- **4231** RUNS
- **205** SIXES
- **121*** HIGHEST SCORE
- **383** FOURS
- **29.73** AVERAGE SCORE
- **65** CATCHES

IPL FORMAT

DECCAN CHARGERS AND MUMBAI INDIANS

272 MATCHES	**132.09** STRIKE RATE
267 INNINGS	**2** CENTURIES
30 NOT OUTS	**47** HALF-CENTURIES
7046 RUNS	**302** SIXES
109* HIGHEST SCORE	**640** FOURS
29.73 AVERAGE SCORE	**102** CATCHES

FEATS

MOST RUNS IN AN INNINGS - ODI	264
MOST HUNDREDS IN A SERIES - ODI	5
MOST RUNS FROM FOURS AND SIXES IN AN INNINGS - ODI	186
MOST MATCHES IN A CAREER - T20I	159
MOST RUNS IN A CAREER - T20I	4231
MOST HUNDREDS IN A CAREER - T20I	5
MOST SIXES IN A CAREER - T20I	205
MOST SIXES IN A CAREER - ALL FORMATS	637

OTHER BOOKS IN THE SERIES

Virat Kohli was obsessed with being no. 1 right from the start. So laser-sharp was his focus that he continued to play cricket even after learning that his dad had died – he was only eighteen! In this action-packed, high-energy book, relive his greatest matches, his record-breaking plays and get inside the mind of a champ who turned challenges into victories, lifted cups and inspired millions. Here's a warning: once you start reading this book, you may just not be able to stop.

Once upon a cricket field, there was a boy named Shubman who loved nothing more than hitting the ball out of the park. In 2018, he helped India win the U19 World Cup and was crowned the best player of the tournament. Just a few years later, he would smash a record-breaking double century in ODIs – becoming the youngest Indian to do so. Now 25, and India's Test and ODI captain, he leads the team he once only dreamed of being a part of. Here's a warning: once you start reading this book, you may just not be able to stop.